DISCOVER
AMERICA

ARKANSAS

Bryan Pezzi

AV² provides enriched content that supplements and complements this book. Weigl's AV² books strive to create inspired learning and engage young minds in a total learning experience.

Your AV² Media Enhanced books come alive with...

Audio
Listen to sections of the book read aloud.

Key Words
Study vocabulary, and complete a matching word activity.

Video
Watch informative video clips.

Quizzes
Test your knowledge.

Go to **www.av2books.com**, and enter this book's unique code.

BOOK CODE

M 2 5 9 3 7 7

Embedded Weblinks
Gain additional information for research.

Slide Show
View images and captions, and prepare a presentation.

AV² by Weigl brings you media enhanced books that support active learning.

Try This!
Complete activities and hands-on experiments.

... and much, much more!

Published by AV² by Weigl
350 5th Avenue, 59th Floor
New York, NY 10118
Website: www.av2books.com

Library of Congress Cataloging-in-Publication Data
Names: Pezzi, Bryan, author.
Title: Arkansas : the natural state / Bryan Pezzi.
Description: New York, NY : AV2 by Weigl, [2016] | Series: Discover America |
 Includes index.
Identifiers: LCCN 2015044633 (print) | LCCN 2015044982 (ebook) | ISBN
 9781489648242 (hard cover : alk. paper) | ISBN 9781489648259 (soft cover :
 alk. paper) | ISBN 9781489648266 (Multi-User eBook)
Subjects: LCSH: Arkansas--Juvenile literature.
Classification: LCC F411.3 .P495 2016 (print) | LCC F411.3 (ebook) | DDC
 976.7--dc23
LC record available at http://lccn.loc.gov/2015044633

Printed in the United States of America, in Brainerd, Minnesotaw
1 2 3 4 5 6 7 8 9 20 19 18 17 16

042016
040816

Project Coordinator Heather Kissock
Art Director Terry Paulhus

ARKANSAS

Contents

STATE TREE
Pine

STATE FLOWER
Apple Blossom

STATE FLAG
Arkansas

ARKANSAS

STATE BIRD
Mockingbird

STATE MAMMAL
White-tailed Deer

STATE SEAL
Arkansas

Nickname
The Natural State

Entered the Union
June 15, 1836, as the 25th state

Song
"Arkansas," by Eva Ware Barnett;
"Arkansas (You Run Deep in Me)," by
Wayland Holyfield; "Oh, Arkansas," by
Terry Rose and Gary Klaff; "The Arkansas
Traveler," words by the Arkansas State Song
Selection Committee, music by
Colonel Sanford Faulkner

Population
(2010 Census) 2,966,369
Ranked 32nd state

Capital
Little Rock

Motto
Regnat Populus
(The People Rule)

Discover Arkansas

Arkansas is known for its Southern charm and natural wonders. The state boasts rugged mountains, clear lakes and streams, and an abundance of wildlife. The southwest is known for its oil fields and grazing cattle, and there are dairy farms and orchards in the northwest. In the east, near the Mississippi River, cotton grows abundantly and is a large part of the area economy.

Arkansas is located in the western portion of the south-central part of the United States, just west of the Mississippi River. Visitors can travel to Arkansas by car, bus, plane, or train. Major transportation routes pass through Little Rock, the state's capital and largest city. Interstates 40 and 30 lead to Little Rock, as do U.S. Highways 65 and 67. Most major domestic airlines touch down and take off at Bill and Hillary Clinton National Airport, which serves about 2.6 million travelers each year.

Arkansas has a strong state university system, with the University of Arkansas, in Fayetteville, one of the fastest growing public research institutions in the country. Outdoor recreation is plentiful, with bass fishing outside of Pine Bluff in the Arkansas River, mountain biking on one of the five trails listed as "epic" by the International Mountain Biking Association, or hiking throughout the vast national forest areas.

The Land

The 4,300-acre Pea Ridge Battlefield is the most well-preserved Civil War battlefield. It stands as a memorial for those who fought and died for their beliefs.

Arkansas's **Hot Spring Mountain** is the source of **47 hot springs**. Their waters reach an average temperature of 143° Fahrenheit.

Arkansas boasts 2.5 million acres of national forest.

Beginnings

The name Arkansas reflects the early influence of Native American and French cultures in the area. French explorers discovered a group of Quapaw Native Americans that they called the Arkansea, a name other local Native Americans used for the Quapaws that means "People of the South Wind." "Arkansea" eventually was modified slightly to "Arkansas." For many years, residents disagreed about how the word should be pronounced. Some people said AR-kan-SAW, while others insisted it was Ar-KANSAS. In 1881, the state's General Assembly decided that the name would be spelled "Arkansas" but pronounced "Arkansaw."

Throughout its history, Arkansas has gained many nicknames in addition to the Natural State. As early as 1875, the state was billed as the Land of Opportunity in an effort to attract new residents. Some people call Arkansas the Hot Water State for its many hot springs.

The capital city of Little Rock has a long and complex history. It took the national spotlight in 1957, when the Little Rock Nine worked to **desegregate** the city's Central High School. The nine students enrolled in the high school were initially prevented from entering the building. During that time, some people wanted to keep Caucasians and African American people separated. In recent years, Little Rock has been a center for government, culture, and education in Arkansas.

The Little Rock Nine, a group of African American students, were at the forefront of the desegregation movement when they were enrolled in Little Rock Central High School amid protest and violence.

Where is
ARKANSAS?

3

Fayetteville

A rkansas is bordered by six other states. In the east, the Mississippi River separates Arkansas from both Tennessee and Mississippi. Missouri lies to the north of Arkansas, and Louisiana lies to the south. Oklahoma and Texas border Arkansas to the west.

OKLAHOMA

United States Map

Arkansas

Alaska   Hawai'i

TEXAS

MAP LEGEND

■ Arkansas

☆ Capital City

● Major City

▧ Crater of Diamonds State Park

☐ Bordering States

☐ Water

N

SCALE 0 —————— 50 miles

---

1 Little Rock

The capital of Arkansas is Little Rock. It is located in Pulaski County on the south bank of the Arkansas River, near the geographical center of the state. Founded in 1821, the city now offers a mix of old and new architecture that includes ornate, nineteenth-century buildings and modern glass-faced skyscrapers.

2 Crater of Diamonds State Park

Located outside of Murfreesboro, Crater of Diamonds State Park is home to one of the largest diamond-bearing volcanic craters in the world. In 1924, the biggest diamond ever found in the United States, at 40.23 carats, was discovered at the park.

MISSOURI

ARKANSAS

Arkansas River

Little Rock

Mississippi River

TENNESSEE

1

4

2

MISSISSIPPI

LOUISIANA

3 Fayetteville

Known as a booming college town, Fayetteville is an economic and cultural hub. Visitors can experience the Clinton House Museum, where President Bill Clinton and Hillary Clinton were married. Fayetteville is also home to the Confederate Cemetery and the Cosmic Cavern, which features underground lakes and rock formations.

4 Arkansas River

The Arkansas River starts in Colorado and flows through Kansas, Oklahoma, and Arkansas. It is a tributary of the Mississippi River and is about 1,460 miles long. The river is home to many recreational activities, including bass fishing and white water rafting.

Land Features

On a map, a diagonal line drawn from St. Francis to Texarkana divides Arkansas into two triangular segments. The lowlands are in the southeast, and the highlands are in the northwest. The low, level plains of the southeast have the best farmland in the state. The northwestern highlands are composed of mountains and deep valleys.

Arkansas has two main mountain ranges. The Ozark Mountains in the north feature dense forests and gurgling rivers and brooks. In western and central Arkansas are the Ouachita Mountains. This area is rich in coal and natural gas. The Arkansas Valley lies between the Ozarks and the Ouachita Mountains.

Ozark Mountains

The Ozark Mountain region is filled with scenic peaks, as well as lush forests, clear-running streams, and a variety of caves and underground caverns.

Lake Chicot

Lake Chicot is the state's largest natural lake. Its name, which means "stump" in French, describes the many cypress tree stumps that line the lake's banks.

Ouachita Mountains

The Ouachita Mountains in western Arkansas are one of two mountain ranges in the country that run east to west, rather than north to south. Visitors to the area can enjoy rugged trails, scenic vistas, and clear lakes.

Magazine Mountain

Magazine Mountain is the state's highest point, at 2,753 feet above sea level. The peak is located in western Arkansas between the Ouachita Mountains and the Ozark Plateau.

Climate

Arkansas's climate is warm and wet. Summers are long and hot, with temperatures occasionally rising above 100° Fahrenheit. Typically, July temperatures soar to about 80°F. Winters are short and mild. January temperatures average about 42°F. Each year, Arkansas averages 51 inches of rainfall and 5 inches of snowfall.

With a varied landscape that includes mountains in the northwest and low-lying plains in the southeast, Arkansas sometimes has weather extremes. These are most common in the spring and fall. In addition, Arkansas's geographic location makes it prone to tornadoes.

Average Annual Precipitation Across Arkansas

The average annual precipitation varies for different areas across Arkansas. How does location affect the amount of precipitation an area receives?

LEGEND

Average Annual Precipitation (in inches) 1961–1990

200 – 100.1

100 – 25.1

25 – 5 and less

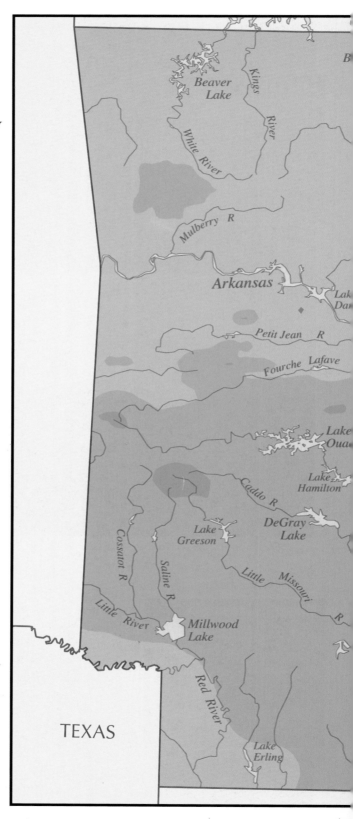

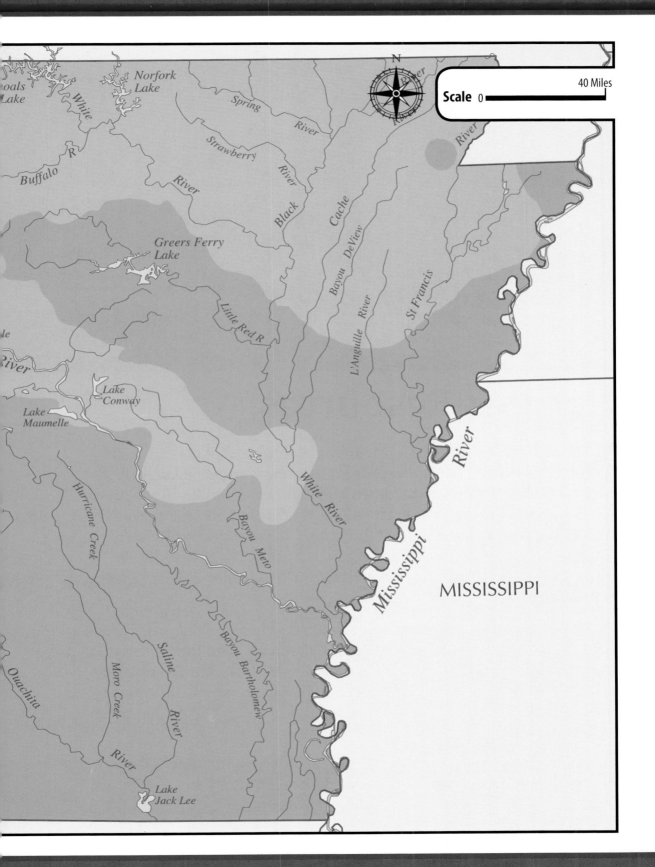

Norfork Lake

oals Lake

White River

Spring River

Strawberry River

Buffalo R

Black River

Cache

Bayou DeView

River

L'Anguille River

St Francis

N

Greers Ferry Lake

Little Red R

River

Lake Conway

Lake Maumelle

White River

Mississippi River

Hurricane Creek

Bayou Meto

MISSISSIPPI

Ouachita

Moro Creek

Saline River

Bayou Bartholomew

River

Lake Jack Lee

Visitors to Crater of Diamonds State Park can walk the rows of dirt, searching for diamonds of their very own.

Nature's Resources

Nature has blessed Arkansas with many resources. Arkansas was the first state to mine diamonds. Diamond mining began in 1906, when John Huddleston spotted two of the glittering stones in the dirt on his farm in southwestern Arkansas. His land became the only diamond mine in the country at the time. Today, visitors can search for diamonds at Crater of Diamonds State Park in Murfreesboro. More than 75,000 diamonds have been found in Crater of Diamonds State Park.

Quartz crystal is another important mineral found in Arkansas. These crystals are sometimes called "Arkansas diamonds," but they are not true diamonds. Quartz crystals are mined in the Ouachita Mountains, and are used in computer components. This stone became Arkansas's state mineral in 1967. Other minerals found in Arkansas include barite and titanium.

Oil and natural gas are both important resources in the state. The production of natural gas has increased during recent years. Petroleum production has decreased but remains significant.

Arkansas quartz is known worldwide as some of the best-quality quartz ever found.

In 2014, Arkansas accounted for more than 4 percent of the natural gas production in the United States.

Vegetation

The Natural State lives up to its nickname. More than half of Arkansas is wooded. Forests and natural areas provide habitats for many plant species.

There are many forested areas in Arkansas's mountains. Hardwood forests of oak, hickory, maple, and beech stretch across the Ozarks. In the Ouachita Mountains, shortleaf pine forests thrive. Pine forests are also common in southern Arkansas.

Arkansas's eastern border is part of the Mississippi Delta region. Swamps and **bayous** support cypress trees and water tupelos. The soil in this area is very fertile, which has led to a large amount of agricultural production.

Many varieties of brightly colored and sweet-smelling flowers bloom in most parts of the state. Passionflowers, water lilies, and orchids grow in Arkansas. There are many different kinds of wildflowers found in the forested areas, including American bellflowers, asters, verbenas, phlox, and wild hydrangeas.

Water Tupelos

Water tupelo trees commonly grow in the swampy and marshy areas of southeastern Arkansas. They can reach a height of 90 feet. The name tupelo comes from a Creek Indian phrase that means "tree and swamp."

Pine Trees

The pine is the state tree. Two varieties, loblolly and shortleaf, are found in the state. Both can grow to be 100 feet tall.

Indian Paintbrushes

Indian paintbrush is a wildflower that is frequently found in rocky areas of the Ozark Mountains. It is also called prairie-fire. The flower usually is a brilliant orange-red color but also can be yellow.

Apple Blossoms

The apple blossom is Arkansas's state flower. It has pink and white petals. At one time, Arkansas was a major apple-producing state.

Wildlife

Arkansas's many natural areas provide homes for a wide variety of animals. Opossums, muskrats, weasels, rabbits, and squirrels can all be found in the state. Red and gray foxes also roam throughout Arkansas. Government game reserves maintain deer and elk populations in the state. The highland regions are home to black bears and bobcats. White-tailed deer and the **endangered** red-cockaded woodpecker live in the pine forests of southern Arkansas.

The wetlands of the Mississippi Delta region, by the state's eastern border, are an important winter haven for migrating birds. The White River National Wildlife **Refuge** provides a winter home for Canada geese and mallard ducks. Some of the birds rest and feed in the fields before flying farther south toward the Gulf of Mexico.

Bobcat

The bobcat, a close relative of the lynx, roams the mountains of Arkansas.

Mockingbird

Arkansas's state bird is the mockingbird. This bird mocks, or imitates, the songs of many other birds.

Red-cockaded Woodpecker

This type of woodpecker is very rare and lives only in old-growth pine forests. It was declared an endangered species in 1970.

White-tailed Deer

The white-tailed deer is the state mammal of Arkansas. This animal raises the white underside of its tail when frightened.

Economy

William J. Clinton Presidential Center and Park

The Clinton Center opened in 2004, in Little Rock. It features a library and museum devoted to Bill Clinton, the 42nd U.S. president.

Tourism

Whether they go to Arkansas to enjoy the great outdoors or to learn about U.S. history, visitors will not be disappointed. The Natural State's many attractions draw about 26 million tourists each year. These visitors spend an average of $6.7 billion annually.

The state capital, Little Rock, is a good place to begin a tour of Arkansas. Little Rock has many historic sites for visitors to enjoy. The Old State House was home to Arkansas's government from 1836 to 1911. Today, the building is a historical museum.

Beyond Little Rock, tourists flock to the mountains to enjoy hiking, camping, and fishing. The Ozark and Ouachita Mountains are especially popular for their beautiful scenery. Arkansas also offers many natural hot springs. Bubbling hot springs can be found in the towns of Eureka Springs and Hot Springs.

Hot Springs National Park

People have been visiting Hot Springs National Park, southwest of Little Rock, for more than 200 years for relaxation and to treat illnesses.

Ouachita National Forest

Located mainly in the mountains of west-central Arkansas, the Ouachita National Forest is the oldest and largest national forest in the South. It covers 1.8 million acres of land.

Old State House Museum

Visitors to Little Rock can see the Old State House Museum, which features exhibits on the state's history.

Arkansas harvests short, medium, and long grain rice.

Primary Industries

Agriculture has always been important to the economy of Arkansas. Watermelons, grapes, blueberries, and apples are all grown in the state. Of all the crops that grow in Arkansas, rice is the most important. Arkansas produces more than twice as much rice as any other state.

In the plains of eastern Arkansas, farmers grow rice in flat fields. Young rice plants must be kept wet. Farmers build earthen banks around their fields and then pump in enough water to cover the plants. The rice plants are submerged under 2 to 6 inches of water until the grain starts to ripen. Then the water is drained, and the rice is harvested.

Chickens are another valuable farm product. Arkansas leads nearly all other states in poultry production. The state's farmers raise more than 1 billion chickens each year. Most are raised for their meat, others for their eggs. Every year, Arkansas chickens produce more than 3 billion eggs.

Pine Bluff, Arkansas is the biggest producer of **archery bows** in the world.

Broiler chickens make up **41%** of the state's livestock production.

In addition to agriculture, Arkansas has a large manufacturing industry. Electrical equipment, chemicals, machinery and other metal products, and goods made of paper, wood, rubber, and plastic are all produced in the state. Other important industries in the state include wholesale and retail trade, finance, insurance, real estate, and professional and technical services. In recent years, the service industry has become increasingly important for the economy.

Value of Goods and Services (in Millions of Dollars)

Manufacturing brings in more money than almost any other sector of Arkansas's economy. Can you name some manufactured products that you use regularly?

Agriculture, forestry, fishing, and hunting $4,261	Finance, and Insurance $4,600
Mining $2,755	Real Estate $12,715
Utilities $2,946	Professional and Business Services $11,067
Construction $4,421	Education $589
Manufacturing $16,410	Healthcare $8,935
Wholesale Trade $8,435	Hotels and Restaurants $3,171
Retail Trade $7,818	Other Services $2,521
Transportation and Warehousing $4,963	Government $15,150
Information $7,796	

The University of Arkansas, founded in 1871, is located in Fayetteville, Arkansas.

Goods and Services

Arkansas's workforce is made up of more than 1.3 million people. Most work in a service job, where they provide a service to other people. This part of the economy is made up of jobs in a great variety of fields, including health care, real estate, trade, and transportation. One important part of the service sector in Arkansas is education. The people who provide educational services include teachers, principals, and college instructors. Arkansas has more than 1,000 public schools and nearly 200 private schools. There are also 24 four-year colleges and 25 two-year colleges. Hospitality and tourism workers provide services, too. They work in restaurants, hotels, and tourist information centers.

In the past, Arkansas's economy relied on agricultural goods. Today, many different types of companies are doing business in the state. Arkansas has the home offices of a number of large companies, including Tyson Foods, Riceland Foods, ALLTEL, Dillard's, and J.B. Hunt Transport Services. Stephens Incorporated, based in Little Rock, is one of the largest financial companies in the country outside New York City.

One of the most famous goods providers in the United States originated in Arkansas. The Wal-Mart chain of stores sells a variety of items, from clothing to toys, to household appliances. The company was founded by Sam Walton, who lived from 1918 to 1992. The first Wal-Mart opened in Rogers, Arkansas, in 1962. By 1991, Wal-Mart had become the largest retail chain in the world.

Tyson Foods processes 41 million chickens every week.

The first Walton's, by the founder of Wal-Mart, opened in Bentonville, Arkansas, in 1950. Today, it is a museum.

Today, Caddo dancers maintain their heritage and culture by dancing at powwows or cultural festivals.

Before the Osage were relocated to Oklahoma, they were semi-nomadic. They moved from place to place, following the animals they hunted.

Native Americans

Archaeologists believe that people have lived in the Arkansas area for at least 12,000 years. The first inhabitants in the area were hunter-gatherers who lived in caves. Later inhabitants of the region were part of the Mississippian culture, which thrived from around the year 800 to the time of European exploration. The Mississippian people built huge earthen mounds and cultivated corn, beans, squash, and other crops. Many of these people lived in towns along rivers.

At the time of European settlement, three main groups of Native Americans lived in the area. The Osage were hunters in northern Arkansas, the Caddo lived along the Red River in the southern part of the state, and the Quapaw built villages at the mouth of the Arkansas River. These peoples grew pumpkins and corn, and hunted wild animals. During the early 1800s, they had to give up much of their land to Caucasian settlers. The government forced the Native Americans to leave Arkansas and other parts of the southeast. Many of them were relocated to a place called "Indian Territory," in what is now Oklahoma.

Exploring the Land

The Spanish explorer Hernando de Soto was the first European to come to the Arkansas region. He arrived in 1541 during an unsuccessful **expedition** for gold. Two Frenchmen, Louis Jolliet and Father Jacques Marquette, visited the area 132 years later. They canoed down the Mississippi River and reached the Arkansas River in 1673. Marquette was a missionary who wanted to teach Christianity to the Native Americans, and Jolliet was a fur trader and mapmaker.

Timeline of Settlement

1682 René-Robert Cavelier, sieur de La Salle, claims the Mississippi Valley for King Louis XIV of France, naming the country "Louisiana."

1686 Arkansas Post is established as a trading post by La Salle's lieutenant, Henri de Tonti.

1673 Louis Jolliet and Father Jacques Marquette travel south on the Mississippi River. They turn back north the next year after reaching the mouth of the Arkansas River.

1762 A secret treaty gives parts of Louisiana, including what is now Arkansas, to Spain. Thirty-eight years later, another secret agreement will return the region to French control.

1541 Spanish conqueror Hernando de Soto leads the first European expedition into Arkansas.

Established as a U.S. Territory

Early Exploration and Colonization

1803 The French government sells the Louisiana Territory to the United States for $15 million. The deal, known as the Louisiana Purchase, makes what is now Arkansas part of the United States.

In 1682, the French explorer René-Robert Cavelier, sieur de La Salle, arrived at the mouth of the Mississippi River. He claimed all of the Mississippi Valley for France. La Salle called this region Louisiana in honor of the king of France, Louis XIV. Arkansas was included in this territory.

La Salle's lieutenant, Henri de Tonti, established the Arkansas Post in 1686. This fur-trading post was the first European settlement in what is now Arkansas. That is why Tonti is known as the Father of Arkansas.

1836 Arkansas becomes the 25th state of the Union on June 15. James Conway is elected its first governor.

1861 Arkansas secedes from, or leaves, the Union and joins the Confederacy.

1861–1865 The people of Arkansas have divided loyalties during the Civil War. Some 50,000 join the Confederate army, while 15,000 fight for the Union.

Statehood and Civil War

1865 The Confederacy is defeated by the Union, and the Civil War ends.

1821 The territorial government moves from Arkansas Post to Little Rock.

1819 President James Monroe signs an act of Congress creating the Territory of Arkansas.

1804–1815 The U.S. government approves various measures to survey and divide the Lousiana Territory and promote settlement of its lands.

1868 Arkansas is readmitted to the Union as a state.

The First Settlers

During the 1700s, European settlement in the Arkansas region was slow to develop. In 1762, France turned over the Louisiana Territory to Spain. The Spanish government offered free land and tax incentives to encourage settlement in the area. Largely unsuccessful in developing the region, Spain returned the territory to France.

In 1803, the United States bought the Louisiana Territory from France. The land that is now Arkansas was included in this deal. In the years that followed, thousands of settlers moved into the Arkansas region. They built log cabins and planted vegetables and fruit trees.

In 1806, Zebulon Pike searched for the Arkansas River. He mapped and explored the area around Arkansas for President Thomas Jefferson.

The Louisiana Purchase was negotiated by Robert Livingston, as appointed by President Thomas Jefferson. At the time, it doubled the amount of land controlled by the United States.

Many settlers farmed in central Arkansas and the northern hills, and some began cultivating apples in the northwest. Others started growing cotton and tobacco in the rich **bottomlands** of the southeast. Many slaves were taken to Arkansas to work on the cotton **plantations** along the Mississippi River. Slavery was legal in the Southern states until the end of the Civil War in 1865.

While most early settlers lived on farms and plantations, new towns began to form as well. Hot Springs was founded in 1807. The town of Fort Smith began as a U.S. Army post in 1817. Arkansas became a territory in 1819. Little Rock was founded the next year, and it became Arkansas's capital in 1821. In 1836, the territory's population reached 60,000 people, the number required for statehood. In that year, Arkansas became the 25th state in the United States.

Early Ozark log cabins were usually just two rooms. An entire family lived and slept in the same space.

History Makers

Many people who were born and lived in Arkansas have made important contributions to the state, the country, and even the world. Arkansas has produced musicians, writers, military personnel, and even a president. Here are just a few Arkansans whose accomplishments had a positive influence on others.

Hattie Caraway (1878–1950)

Caraway was a Jonesboro resident when her husband, Thaddeus, became a U.S. senator in 1921. When he died in 1931, Hattie was appointed by Arkansas's governor to fill the position. After winning a special election in 1932, she became the first woman ever elected to the U.S. Senate. She spent 13 years in Congress.

Douglas MacArthur (1880–1964)

Born in Little Rock, MacArthur was one of the most famous U.S. generals of the twentieth century. He helped lead the U.S. and its allies to victory in the Pacific during World War II. MacArthur also commanded U.S. troops in the Korean War, until dismissed by President Harry Truman for publicly disagreeing with Truman's policies.

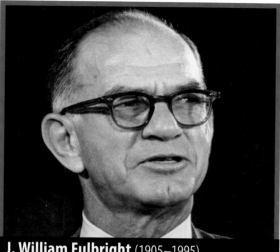

J. William Fulbright (1905–1995)

Fulbright, who grew up in Fayetteville, spent almost 30 years as a U.S. senator. During that time, he became known for promoting cultural tolerance and international cooperation. In 1946, he established the Fulbright scholarship program, which allows American students and educators to study abroad.

John H. Johnson (1918–2005)

Johnson was born in Arkansas City, but moved to Chicago before he began high school. In 1942, he founded the Johnson Publishing Company, which has become the largest African American–owned media company in the world. It publishes two very popular African American–oriented magazines, *Ebony* and *Jet*.

Bill Clinton (1946–)

Clinton was born in Hope, Arkansas, and grew up in Hot Springs. In 1978, he became governor of Arkansas at age 32, making him the youngest person ever to be elected a U.S. governor. Clinton was elected the 42nd president of the United States in 1992 and served two terms. Following his presidency, Clinton has served his country as a diplomat, statesman, and philanthropist.

Culture

Eureka Springs is home to the Fat Tire Mountain Festival, which celebrates the outdoor enthusiast culture of the state.

Little Rock, Arkansas, was named *Forbes'* Cleanest City in 2011. It also won *Outside Magazine's* Best City in 2013.

The People Today

With more than 2.9 million people, Arkansas is the 32nd largest state in population. Arkansas has always been an agricultural state, with a great number of people living in **rural** areas. About 40 percent of the population live on farms or in other rural settings.

Most of the cities in Arkansas are small. Little Rock is the largest city in Arkansas, with a population of more than 197,000. As the state capital, Little Rock is a center for government, education, transportation, and culture. Little Rock also has a "twin city" across the Arkansas River. This city, North Little Rock, has a population of almost 66,000. Other major cities in Arkansas include Fort Smith, Pine Bluff, Fayetteville, Springdale, Jonesboro, and Hot Springs.

Arkansas's population **increased** by **more than 565,000** people from **2000 to 2010.**

Q What are some of the reasons that many people from other states and other countries are choosing to move to Arkansas?

State Government

Laws and important decisions that affect all Arkansans are made in Little Rock. The state government is composed of three branches. The executive branch approves and administers laws. The legislative branch introduces new laws and changes existing ones. The judicial branch is composed of the state courts.

The state legislature, or General Assembly, consists of the Senate and the House of Representatives. The Senate has 35 members, and the House of Representatives has 100. On the federal level, two senators and four members of the House of Representatives represent Arkansas in the U.S. Congress in Washington, D.C.

Bill Clinton is a well-known political figure from Arkansas. He was elected governor of Arkansas in 1978 and served the state in this role for many years. Clinton then served as the president of the United States from 1993 to 2001. Another notable Arkansas politician is Mike Huckabee. He was governor from 1996 to 2007, and unsuccessfully competed for the Republican presidential nomination in 2008.

As of 2015, the Arkansas General Assembly is on its 90th session.

The Arkansas capitol building was constructed from 1899 to 1915, making it more than 100 years old.

Mike Huckabee served as Arkansas's governor for 11 years, becoming one of the longest-serving governors in the state's history.

Arkansas has four state songs. One of these, "Arkansas" by Eva Ware Barnett, was designated the state's official anthem in 1987.

"Arkansas."

I am thinking tonight of the Southland,
Of the home of my childhood days,
Where I roamed through the
woods and the meadows,
By the mill and the brook that plays

Arkansas, Arkansas, 'tis a name dear,
Tis the place I call "home, sweet home,"
Arkansas, Arkansas, I salute thee,
From thy shelter no more I'll roam

* excerpted

The Ozark Folk Center State Park works to preserve the culture of the people who settled in the Ozark Mountains.

Celebrating Culture

About four-fifths of Arkansans are of European heritage. European settlers arrived in the state from Ireland, Germany, Great Britain, and many other countries. Some of these newcomers settled in the Ozark Mountains. They created a rich folk culture with their own arts, crafts, music, and dances. They were **resourceful** and made many things by hand instead of buying them. The Ozark Folk Center in Mountain View works to preserve the cultural traditions of this region. Local musicians may be seen at the Ozark Folk Center playing folk songs on the traditional instruments of this musical style, including fiddles, banjos, and guitars.

The Ozark Folk Center Crafts Village features a variety of trades important to the history of the Ozarks. Pottery, basket weaving, broom making, and soap making are just a few crafts exhibited.

African Americans are another important cultural group in Arkansas, making up slightly more than 15 percent of the population. When the first Africans were taken to Arkansas in the late 1700s, most of them were forced to work as slaves on plantations. This continued until slavery was outlawed in the United States as a result of the Civil War. Every February, Arkansas celebrates Black History Month. This is a time for African Americans to share and preserve their history and culture. Many people reflect on African Americans' long struggle for civil rights in the United States.

At the time of European settlement, a number of Native American groups lived in the Arkansas area. Many Native Americans were forced to move out of the region in the years leading up to statehood in 1836. Today, Native Americans account for only a small number of the state's residents. In total, there are some 22,000 Native Americans living in Arkansas.

The Northwest Arkansas International Festival is held annually in Rogers, Arkansas. More than 50 countries are represented each year. Cultural dancing, musical performances, and a variety of ethnic foods can be enjoyed.

Johnny Cash is best known for combining gospel and country sounds with rock and roll.

Arts and Entertainment

Arkansas boasts a thriving arts scene. Many people in the state use art, music, and the written word to share their ideas and experiences with others. Colleges and folk centers in the state promote the arts.

Country music is a prominent part of Arkansas's arts and entertainment scene. Many well-known artists have come from the state. Johnny Cash, born in Kingsland, was a very popular and influential singer. His hits included "I Walk the Line" and "Folsom Prison Blues." Conway Twitty was called the High Priest of Country Music. He was raised in Helena, where he was known as Harold Jenkins. His stage name combines the names of two towns, Conway, Arkansas, and Twitty, Texas.

The Great Passion Play in Eureka Springs, Arkansas, is the **#1 attended** outdoor drama in the United States.

The **FIDDLE** is Arkansas's state instrument.

Arkansas also has produced famous musicians who are known for other styles of music. Ne-Yo is a chart-topping R&B artist who sings, raps, and dances. He was born in Camden, and his given name is Shaffer Chimere Smith. Forrest City native Al Green is a renowned soul and gospel singer. Louis Jordan was a pioneer of jazz, blues, and R&B. He was born in Brinkley.

Singer and song writer Ne-Yo is a three-time Grammy award winner.

Some acclaimed writers also have come from Arkansas. John Grisham, who was born in Jonesboro, writes legal thrillers. His many novels include *The Firm, The Pelican Brief,* and *The Client.* Maya Angelou, who grew up in Stamps, has won national recognition as a poet, novelist, actress, educator, and civil-rights activist. She is best known for her book *I Know Why the Caged Bird Sings*, which tells of her childhood experiences in Arkansas.

Arkansas offers numerous cultural attractions. Little Rock has many of the state's theaters, museums, and musical venues. The Arkansas Symphony, Ballet Arkansas, and the Arkansas Arts Center are all based in Little Rock.

Maya Angelou was awarded the Medal of Freedom by President Obama in 2010. It is the highest civilian award in the U.S. and is only bestowed by an act of Congress.

Sports and Recreation

With its mountains, streams, and beautiful scenery, the Natural State is the perfect place for outdoor sports and activities. Arkansas has more than 200 public campgrounds and many more private ones. There are countless day hikes, mountain bike paths, and **equestrian** trails to enjoy. People can even explore underground caves. Serious hikers can take an extended backpacking trip on the Ozark Highlands National Recreation Trail.

Bikers will enjoy touring the mountains and valleys of northern Arkansas. This region has some of the most scenic and physically challenging bike tours in the United States. Bikers can also explore bike routes in the Mississippi Valley. They will find both hills and level stretches in this area.

Mt. Magazine is the state's tallest mountain at 2,753 feet. The state park where it is located is a haven for outdoor adventurers.

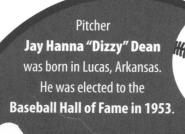

Pitcher **Jay Hanna "Dizzy" Dean** was born in Lucas, Arkansas. He was elected to the **Baseball Hall of Fame in 1953**.

Stuttgart, Arkansas, is home to the annual World Championship **Duck Calling Contest**.

Fishing and hunting are also popular pastimes in Arkansas. People can travel the more than 9,000 miles of streams in the state by canoe, **johnboat**, or raft. Known as a fisher's haven, these waterways provide some of the world's best fishing. Bass, walleye, and many kinds of trout are found in them.

Many people take advantage of the golf courses found all over Arkansas. Golfers can find courses in the mountains and in the delta region. Because of the warm climate, golfers in Arkansas can tee off year-round.

Many Arkansans enjoy watching and playing team sports. The University of Arkansas sports teams are known as the Razorbacks, after a type of wild hog native to the area. Football is especially

The White River features some of the best trout fishing in the area.

popular in the state. The Razorbacks football team has won many postseason games, including the Orange Bowl, the Sugar Bowl, and the Cotton Bowl. The Razorbacks men's basketball team won the national title in 1994.

The Arkansas Razorbacks have sent many players to the National Football League. In 2015, they had five players drafted by three different NFL teams.

Get To Know
ARKANSAS

With a total area of **53,179 SQUARE MILES,** Arkansas is the **29th largest state.**

The town of Alma, Arkansas, claims to be the **spinach capital** of the world.

It is **illegal** to mispronounce "Arkansas" while in the state.

In 1985, **milk** became Arkansas's official beverage.

Magnolia, Arkansas is home to the **world's largest charcoal grill**. Every year the town hosts the World Championship Steak Cook-off.

Stuttgart is known as the
RICE AND DUCK
Capital of the World.

Hope, Arkansas, is best known for being the home of a **watermelon** that weighed more than **100 pounds**.

Brain Teasers

What have you learned about Arkansas after reading this book? Test your knowledge by answering these questions. All of the information can be found in the text you just read. The answers are provided below for easy reference.

1 What is Arkansas's official nickname?

2 What is the capital of Arkansas?

3 What are the two main mountain regions in Arkansas?

4 Arkansas was the first state to mine which mineral?

5 What is Arkansas's most important crop?

6 Who was the first European to come to the region now known as Arkansas?

7 Which United States president was born in Hope, Arkansas?

8 Which famous country singer was born in Arkansas and had hit songs that included "I Walk the Line" and "Folsom Prison Blues"?

ANSWER KEY
1. The Natural State 2. Little Rock 3. Ozark Mountains and Ouachita Mountains 4. Diamonds 5. Rice 6. Hernando de Soto 7. Bill Clinton 8. Johnny Cash

Key Words

bayous: marshy arms of a lake or river

bottomlands: low-lying lands around a waterway

desegregate: reversal of forced separation and restrictions based on race

endangered: in danger of dying out

equestrian: involving horses or horseback riding

expedition: a journey of exploration

johnboat: a narrow, flat-bottomed boat used on rivers and streams

plantations: large farms that are usually tended by resident workers

refuge: place of shelter and protection

resourceful: able to invent new ways to do or make things in difficult situations

rural: of or relating to life in the country or on farms

Index

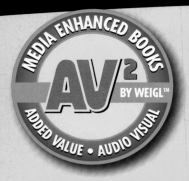

Log on to www.av2books.com

AV² by Weigl brings you media enhanced books that support active learning. Go to www.av2books.com, and enter the special code found on page 2 of this book. You will gain access to enriched and enhanced content that supplements and complements this book. Content includes video, audio, weblinks, quizzes, a slide show, and activities.

AV² Online Navigation

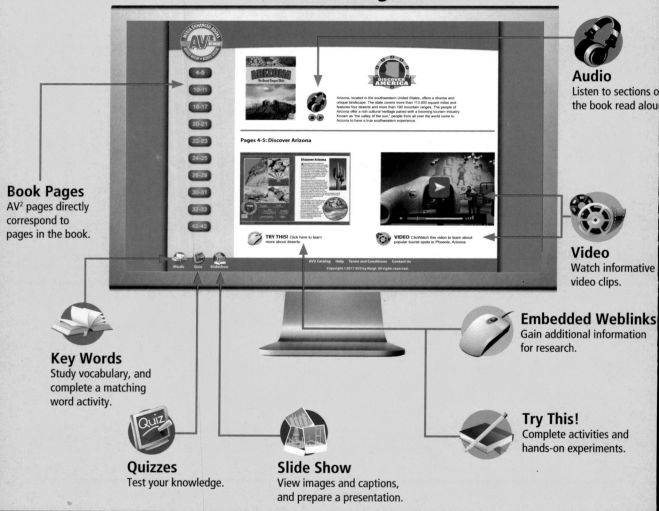

Audio
Listen to sections of the book read aloud

Book Pages
AV² pages directly correspond to pages in the book.

Video
Watch informative video clips.

Key Words
Study vocabulary, and complete a matching word activity.

Embedded Weblinks
Gain additional information for research.

Try This!
Complete activities and hands-on experiments.

Quizzes
Test your knowledge.

Slide Show
View images and captions, and prepare a presentation.

AV² was built to bridge the gap between print and digital. We encourage you to tell us what you like and what you want to see in the future.

Sign up to be an AV² Ambassador at www.av2books.com/ambassador.

Due to the dynamic nature of the Internet, some of the URLs and activities provided as part of AV² by Weigl may have changed or ceased to exist. AV² by Weigl accepts no responsibility for any such changes. All media enhanced books are regularly monitored to update addresses and sites in a timely manner. Contact AV² by Weigl at 1-866-649-3445 or av2books@weigl.com with any questions, comments, or feedback.